FOR:

LOUISA MAY ALCOTT'S
LITTLE INSTRUCTION BOOK

COMPILED BY

EVELYN L. BEILENSON AND LOIS L. KAUFMAN

DESIGN BY LESLEY EHLERS

PETER PAUPER PRESS, INC.
WHITE PLAINS, NEW YORK

Special thanks to Robert A. Feldman
for assistance in compilation

Jacket inset illustration by Louis Jambor reprinted by permission of Grosset & Dunlap, Inc. from Little Women by Louisa May Alcott, copyright © 1947, © renewed 1975 by Grosset & Dunlap, Inc.
Photograph on page 4, and illustrations on the endpaper, and on pp. 1, 3, 5, 6, 7, 9, 13, 16, 17, 34, 48, 59, 61, and 64, courtesy of The Louisa May Alcott Memorial Association (available for viewing at Orchard House, Home of the Alcotts, Concord, MA).

Peter Pauper Press, Inc.
202 Mamaroneck Avenue
White Plains, NY 10601

ISBN 0-88088-694-3
Printed in China
7 6 5 4 3 2

Contents

Louisa May Alcott

Introduction

This little instruction book is like a string of pearls—beautiful sentiments and observations chosen from the pages of Louisa May Alcott's enduring novels, *Little Women*, *Little Men*, and *Jo's Boys*.

Alcott's stories, with characters drawn from her own family, reflect her passion for life. Her "pearls" of wisdom and insight—

whether she's writing about love, friendship, women, self-image, or spirituality–have as much meaning today as when they were drawn from her nineteenth-century New England vantage point.

Like most women I know, my sisters and I (we are three– so we elected a friend to be the fourth sister) identify with Amy, Meg, Beth and Jo. We cannot agree, however, on which of us personifies each of the March sisters, but we care passionately for those girls and the women they became.

Like Jo, I always wanted to write. When I was ten I wrote plays, poetry, and journals. I had an inner voice that yearned to be free. I wept during the scene when Jo unwraps the galley of her book. I felt the strength of a writer's passion. Just like Jo.

No matter which of Miss Alcott's characters draws you in, you'll find a marvelous world that will make you want to dip, time and again, into the inner lives of these women.

Patricia Eisemann

Life Lessons

A holiday isn't a holiday, without plenty of freedom and fun.

Little Men, Mrs. Bhaer

Liberty must not be abused.

Little Men

If you exercise your mind, it will get hungry just as your body does.

Little Men, Mr. Bhaer

Salt is like good-humor, and nearly every thing is better for a pinch of it.

Little Men, Mr. Bhaer

[One] must wait a little, learn self-control, and be ready to use her freedom before she asked for it.

Little Men

Simple, genuine goodness is the best capital to found the business of this life upon. It lasts when fame and money fail, and is the only riches we can take out of this world with us.

Little Men, Mr. Bhaer

Our burdens are here, our road is before us, and the longing for goodness and happiness is the guide that leads us through many troubles and mistakes . . .

Little Women, Marmee

Men always croak when they are hungry.

Little Women, Jo

I've been trying to cure it [anger] for forty years, and have only succeeded in controlling it. I am angry nearly every day of my life, Jo, but I have learned not to show it; and I still hope to learn not to feel it, though it may take me another forty years to do so.

Little Women, Marmee

Have regular hours for work and play, make each day both useful and pleasant, and prove that you understand the worth of time by employing it well. Then youth will be delightful, old age will bring few regrets, and life become a beautiful success, in spite of poverty.

Little Women, Marmee

"Hope and keep busy," that's the motto for us . . .

Little Women, Jo

Gentlemen, which means boys, be courteous to the old maids, no matter how poor and plain and prim, for the only chivalry worth having is that which is the readiest to pay deference to the old, protect the feeble, and serve womankind, regardless of rank, age, or color.

Little Women

Aim at the highest, and never mind the money.

Little Women, Mr. March

To the inspiration of necessity, we owe half the wise, beautiful, and useful blessings of the world.

Little Women

The homeliest tasks get beautified if loving hands do them.

Little Women

The treasures of real home love and mutual helpfulness . . . the poorest may possess, and the richest cannot buy.

Little Women

I do think people ought to see their own country before they go scooting off to foreign parts, as if the new world wasn't worth discovering.

Jo's Boys, Dan

Power is a dangerous thing. Be careful that you don't abuse it or let it make a tyrant of you.

Jo's Boys, Mrs. Jo

Now and then genius carries all before it, but not often. We have to climb slowly, with many slips and falls.

Jo's Boys, Miss Cameron

Chance words spoken in kindness often help amazingly; and that's what old people are here for—else their experience is of little use.

Jo's Boys, Mrs. Jo

Women

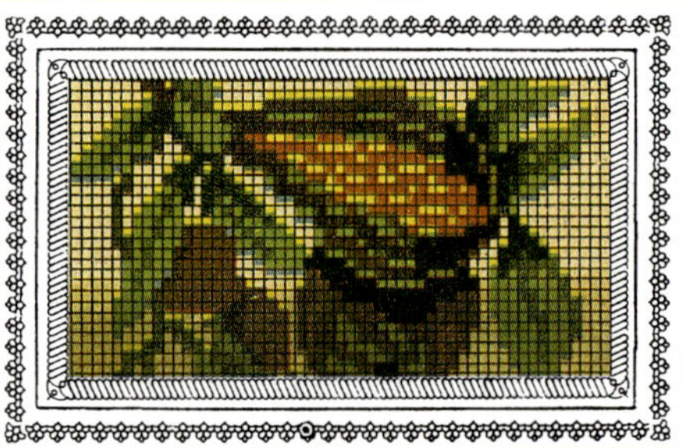

The female population exceeds the male, you know, especially in New England, which accounts for the high state of culture we are in, perhaps.

Jo's Boys, John

It takes three or four women to get each man into, through, and out of the world.

Jo's Boys, Mrs. Jo

It is well that mothers, sisters, wives, and daughters love their duty and do it so well, or you [men] would perish off the face of the earth.

Jo's Boys, Mrs. Jo

Men are always ready to die for us, but not to make our lives worth having.

Jo's Boys, Nan

Few women, even the most learned, are without that desire to look well which makes many a plain face comely, as well as many a pretty one ugly for want of skill and knowledge of the fitness of things.

Jo's Boys

[Girls] will soon show what they want, if they are let alone, and not all run in the same mold.

Jo's Boys, Mrs. Jo

A real lady is always known by neat boots, gloves, and handkerchief.

Little Women, Meg

Better be happy old maids than unhappy wives, or unmaidenly girls, running about to find husbands . . .

Little Women, Marmee

Young ladies in America love independence as much as their ancestors did, and are admired and respected for supporting themselves.

Little Women, Mr. Brooke

I want my daughters to be beautiful, accomplished, and good; to be admired, loved, and respected; to have a happy youth, to be well and wisely married, and to lead useful, pleasant lives, with as little care and sorrow to try them as God sees fit to send.

Little Women, Marmee

Don't laugh at the spinsters, dear girls, for often very tender, tragic romances are hidden away in the hearts that beat so quietly under the sober gowns, and many silent sacrifices of youth, health, ambition, love itself, make the faded faces beautiful in God's sight.

Little Women

Girls could do most things as well as boys, and some things better.

Little Men

Money

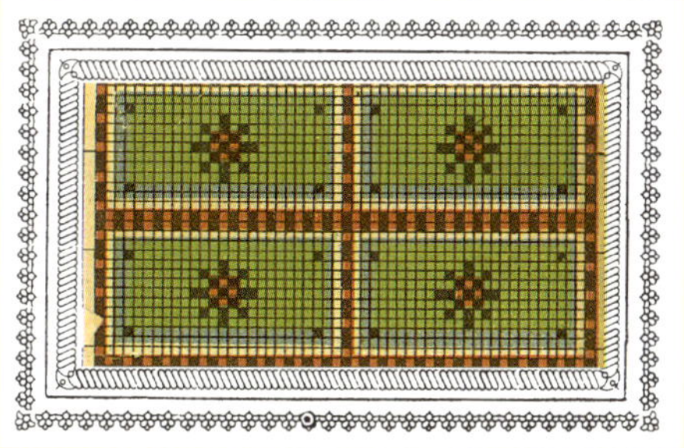

Money is the root of all evil, and yet it is such a useful root that we cannot get on without it any more than we can without potatoes.

Little Men

Money couldn't keep shame and sorrow out of rich people's houses . . .

Little Women, Marmee

Money is a needful and precious thing—and, when well used, a noble thing—but I never want you to think it is the first or only prize to strive for.

Little Women, Marmee

Prosperity suits some people, and they blossom best in a glow of sunshine; others need the shade, and are the sweeter for a touch of frost.

Jo's Boys

Time is money, peace is health . . .

Jo's Boys, Mrs. Jo

We don't care for money; but a long line of virtuous ancestors *is* something to desire and to be proud of.

Jo's Boys, Mrs. Jo

Love

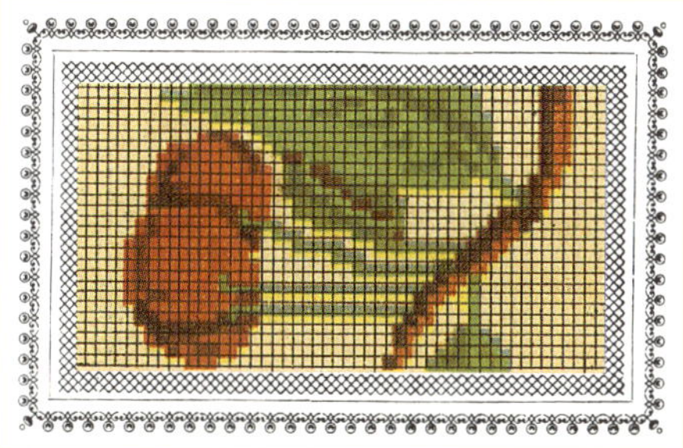

Love is apt to make lunatics of even saints and sages.

Jo's Boys

Love casts out fear, and gratitude can conquer pride.

Little Women

Poverty seldom daunts a sincere lover.

Little Women, Marmee

I never knew how much like heaven this world could be, when two people love and live for one another!

Little Women, Amy

Honesty is the best policy in love as in law . . .

Little Women

Where the heart is the mind works best.

Little Men

The warmth of love and care [is] the best climate for young hearts and souls all the world over.

Little Men

Love is a flower that grows in any soil, works its sweet miracles undaunted by autumn frost or winter snow, blooming fair and fragrant all the year, and blessing those who give and those who receive.

Little Men

Self-Image

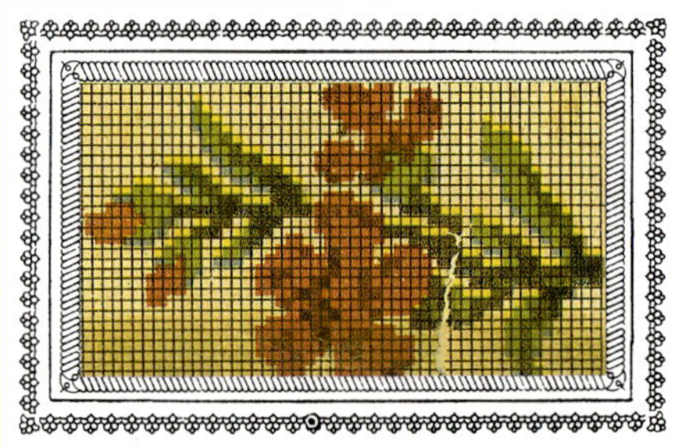

[To be good] is hard work sometimes.

Little Men, Mrs. Bhaer

[Accomplishments and elegance] are always seen and felt in a person's manner and conversation, if modestly used, but it is not necessary to display them.

Little Women, Marmee

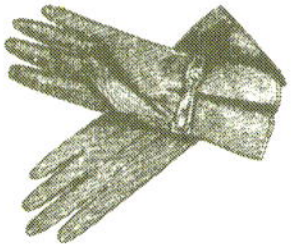

Conceit spoils the finest genius.

Little Women, Marmee

Learn to know and value the praise which is worth having, and to excite the admiration of excellent people by being modest as well as pretty, Meg.

Little Women, Marmee

The love of power . . . sleeps in the bosoms of the best of little women . . .

Little Women

People cannot be molded like clay.

Jo's Boys

We must each be what God and nature make us. We can't change it much—only help to develop the good and control the bad elements in us.

Jo's Boys, Demi

We don't choose our talents but we needn't hide them in a napkin because they are not just what we want.

Jo's Boys, Mrs. Meg

Think of the persons whom you respect most, and in imitating them you will secure the respect of those who look up to you.

Jo's Boys, Mrs. Jo

Work

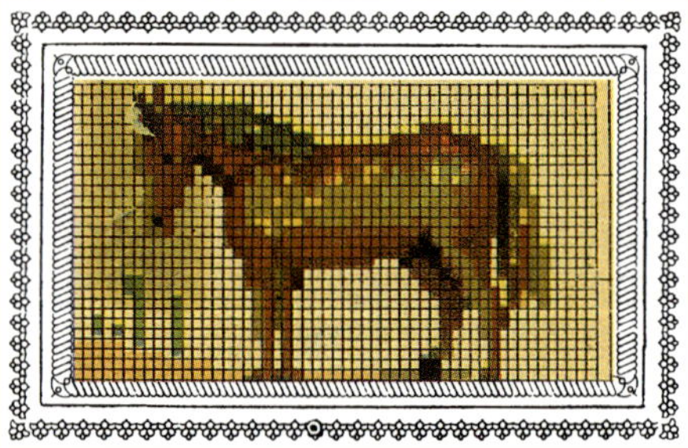

It adds so much to one's happiness to love the task one does.

Jo's Boys, Mrs. Meg

Have your fun, my dear; but if you must earn your bread, try to make it sweet with cheerfulness, not bitter with the daily regret that it isn't cake.

Jo's Boys, Mrs. Jo

Work is wholesome, and there is plenty for everyone; it keeps us from ennui and mischief, is good for health and spirits, and gives us a sense of power and independence better than money or fashion.

Little Women, Marmee

Love duty for its own sake, and try to do it faithfully, [and] sooner or later the recompense would come.

Little Men

Relationships

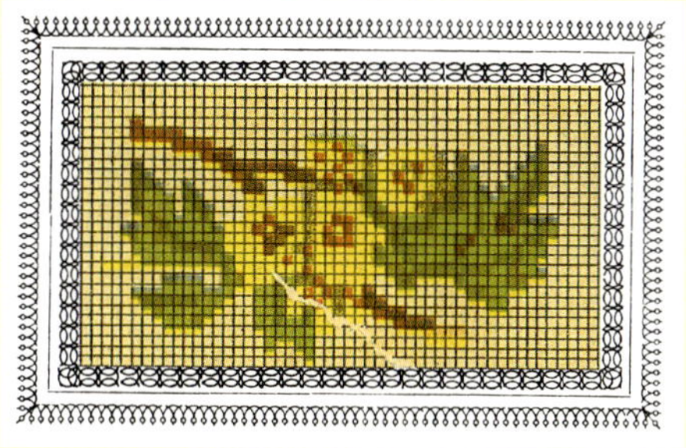

Kindness in looks and words and ways is true politeness, and any one can have it if they only try to treat other people as they like to be treated themselves.

Little Men, Mrs. Bhaer

If men and women would only trust, understand, and help one another as . . . children do, what a capital place the world would be!

Little Men, Mrs. Bhaer

Sympathy is a sweet thing.

Little Men

If little men are like big ones, good cooking will touch their hearts and soothe their tempers delightfully.

Little Men, Mrs. Bhaer

We can't begin too soon to try to understand the needs, virtues, and failings of those nearest us. Love should not make us blind to faults, nor familiarity make us too ready to blame the shortcomings we see.

Jo's Boys, Mrs. Jo

Marriage, they say, halves one's rights and doubles one's duties.

Little Women, Laurie

Young people think they never can change, but they do in the most wonderful manner, and very few die of broken hearts.

Jo's Boys, Mrs. Jo

Parenting

No false delicacy should keep [parents] from the watchful care, the gentle warning, which makes self-knowledge and self-control the compass and pilot of the young as they leave the safe harbor of home.

Jo's Boys

Mothers can forgive *anything!*

Jo's Boys, Mrs. Jo

Mother love [is] that divine gift which comforts, purifies, and strengthens all who seek it.

Jo's Boys

Fathers should have their share in the education of both girls and boys . . .

Jo's Boys, Mrs. Jo

Mothers have need of sharp eyes and discreet tongues when they have girls to manage.

Little Women, Marmee

The natural refinement which nothing but home influence can teach, gave him sweet and simple manners.

Little Men

No matter how lost and soiled and worn-out wandering sons may be, mothers can forgive and forget every thing as they fold them in their fostering arms.

Little Men

It is never too early to try and plant [good principles] in a child, and never too late to cultivate them in the most neglected person.

Little Men, Mrs. Bhaer

Morality

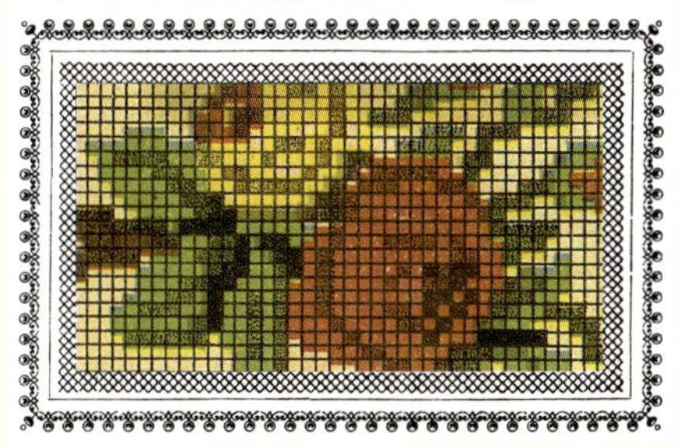

A lie is a lie, and though we all tell many polite untruths in this queer world of ours, it is not right, and everybody knows it.

Little Men

Charity is an excellent foundation to build anything upon.

Little Men

Sweet satisfaction . . . comes to those who try, no matter how humbly, to be earthly providences to the poor and helpless, and gild their mite with the gold of charity before it is laid up where thieves cannot break through and steal.

Little Men

Trials and temptations . . . beset all lives in the beginning, and so often mar them, for want of the right word at the right moment.

Jo's Boys

Virtue, which means honor, honesty, courage, and all that makes character, is the red thread that marks a good man wherever he is.

Jo's Boys, Mrs. Jo

Temperance in all things is the only safe rule.

Jo's Boys, Mrs. Jo

You can be a gentleman in the true sense of the word; and no matter what happens to your body, keep your soul clean, your heart true to those who love you, and do your duty to the end.

Jo's Boys, Mrs. Jo

Spirituality

Better lose your life than your soul.

Jo's Boys, Mrs. Jo

There is no other help or hope for human weakness but God's love and patience.

Jo's Boys, Mrs. Jo

Don't let false shame make you neglect the religion without which no man can live. You needn't talk about it if you don't like, but don't shut your heart to it in whatever shape it comes.

Jo's Boys, Mrs. Jo

There is hope and help for everyone, for God's mercy is infinite and man's charity is great; but penitence and submission must come before the cure is possible.

Jo's Boys, Preacher

There is more rejoicing over one repentant sinner than many saints.

Jo's Boys, Mrs. Jo